THE PERFECT SLIME

THIS BOOK BELONGS TO:
_____

©Copyright

By: Saffia Abdul-Haqq

In a world so bright and a room so neat,

Kids mix slime, a colorful treat.

Start with glue, just a little pour,

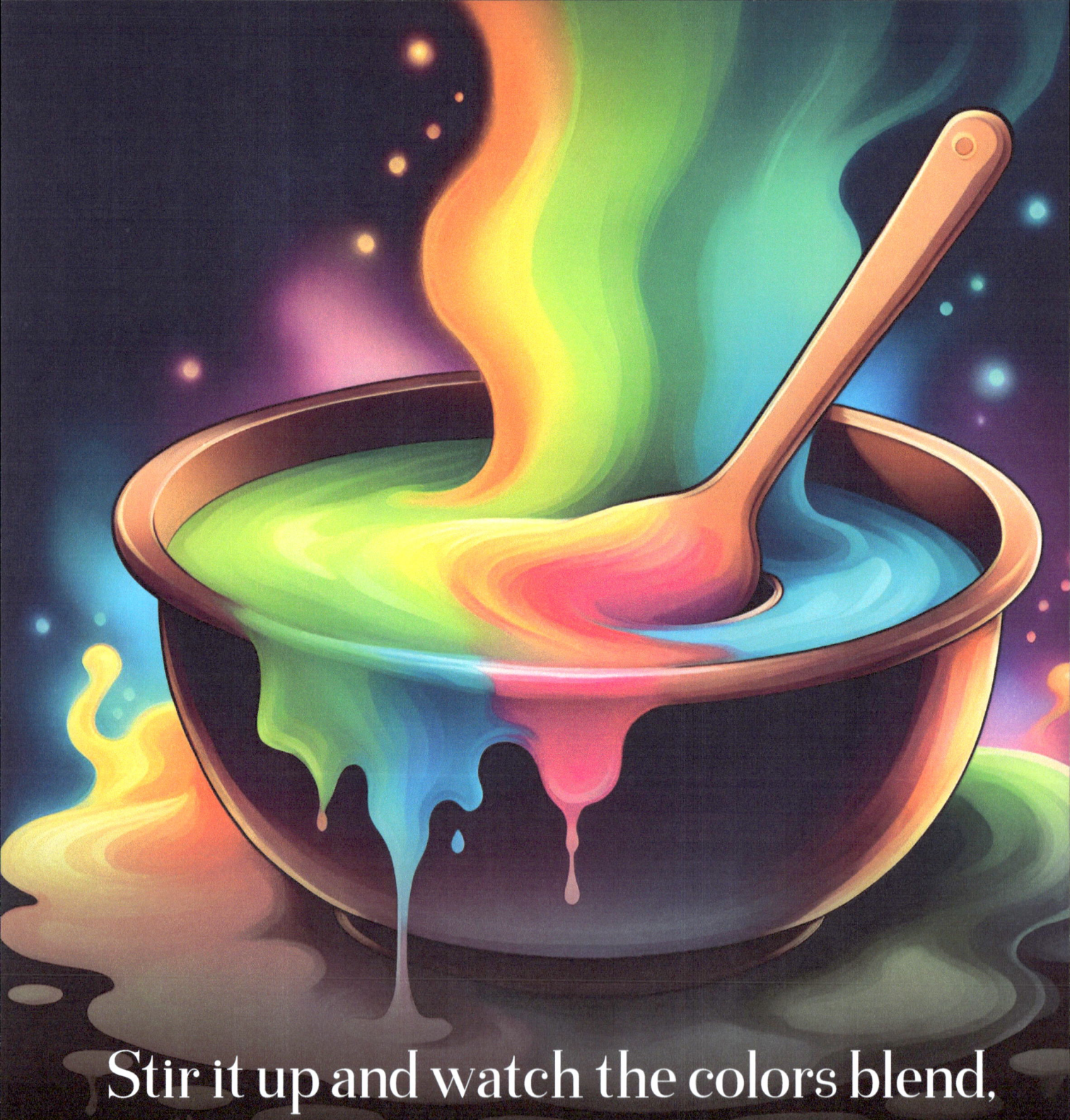

Stir it up and watch the colors blend,

The fun with slime never ends.

A lot of fun, and a little bit of time.

Mix it up and then see slime.

Squishy, stretchy, soft and clear,

Playing with slime brings joy and cheer.

Watch it jiggle, watch it sway,

Pull it, twist it, make it dance,

Add some sparkles, shiny and bright,

Glittery slime is pure delight.

Soft as a cloud, smooth as a dream,

Playing with slime is as fun as it seems.

Try some scents, sweet or zesty,

Mix and match to find the best,

Your perfect slime beats all the rest.

In your hands, it's squishy fun,

A playful race that's always won.

Share your slime with friends who care,

In the world of slime, you'll find your way,

To make the perfect slime today!

www.ingramcontent.com/pod-product-compliance
Lightning Source LLC
Chambersburg PA
CBHW041525070526
44585CB00002B/86